FAITHFUL CITIZEN, FAITHFUL CATHOLIC

FAITHFUL CITIZEN, FAITHFUL CATHOLIC

Informing Your Conscience and Your Vote

Fr. Michael J. McDermott

Saint Mary's Press®

Dedication

To my parents, John and Jean, who first taught me what it means to be among you as one who serves.

The publishing team included Steven C. McGlaun, development editor; Lorraine Kilmartin, reviewer; iStockphoto / Nicholas Monu, cover photo; prepress and manufacturing coordinated by the production departments of Saint Mary's Press.

Copyright © 2007 by Fr. Michael J. McDermott. All rights reserved. No part of this book may be reproduced by any means without the written permission of the publisher, Saint Mary's Press, Christian Brothers Publications, 702 Terrace Heights, Winona, MN 55987-1318, www.smp.org.

Printed in the United States of America

ISBN 978-0-88489-980-8

1349

Library of Congress Cataloging-in-Publication Data

McDermott, Michael J.
    Faithful citizen, faithful Catholic : informing your conscience and your vote / Michael J. McDermott.
    p. cm.
ISBN 978-0-88489-980-8 (pbk.)
    1. Christianity and politics—Catholic Church. 2. Catholic Church—Doctrines. 3. Catholics—Political activity. I. Title.

BX1793.M36 2007
261.7088'282—dc22

2007013589

Contents

Introduction 6

Chapter 1: The Church Community 9
    Growth in Virtue as an Individual and as a Member of a Community
    Informing Your Conscience
    Violence and Peace
    Promoting Peace Through Politics

Chapter 2: You Are God's Beloved: The Dignity of the Human Person .13
    Guiding Vision
    The Family
    Beginning of Life
    End of Life

Chapter 3: You Are God's Beloved People: The Common Good. . . . 20
    Guiding Vision
    The Common Good
    Community Challenges
    Political Issues
    Economic Issues
    Cultural Issues

Chapter 4: Making Decisions 31
    Social Teachings of the Catholic Church
    Whom to Vote For? What Ballot Issues to Vote For?
    Making Moral Decisions
    Questions and Answers
    The Long Haul

Acknowledgments 38

Introduction
In the Steps of Jesus

> Then one of the leaders of the synagogue named Jairus came and, when he saw him [Jesus], fell at his feet and begged him repeatedly, "My little daughter is at the point of death. Come and lay your hands on her, so that she may be made well, and live." So he went with him.
> And a large crowd followed him and pressed in on him.
> . . . Some people came from the leader's house to say, "Your daughter is dead. Why trouble the teacher any further?" But overhearing what they said, Jesus said to the leader of the synagogue, "Do not fear, only believe." He allowed no one to follow him except Peter, James, and John, the brother of James. When they came to the house of the leader of the synagogue, he saw a commotion, people weeping and wailing loudly. When he had entered, he said to them, "Why do you make a commotion and weep? The child is not dead but sleeping." And they laughed at him. Then he put them all outside, and took the child's father and mother and those who were with him, and went in where the child was. He took her by the hand and said to her, "Talithacum," which means, "Little girl, get up!" And immediately the girl got up and began to walk about (she was twelve years of age). At this they were overcome with amazement. (Mark 5:22–24,35–43)

Jesus embodied God's power to bring new life, to be a healing presence in the face of suffering and even death. He also empowered his disciples and sent them to share in his healing work.

We Are Called

"Then Jesus called the twelve together and gave them power and authority over all demons and to cure diseases, and he sent them out to proclaim the kingdom of God and to heal" (Luke 9:1–2).

Jesus taught his disciples how to become a light that would lead others to new life, and he empowered them to do so. The Bible describes this new life as a city with a river of sparkling crystal water. On each bank of the river, trees of life grow with leaves that serve as healing medicine for the nations (see Revelation 21:1–4, 22:1–2). What does all this mean? It means God is calling each of us to become God's partner in building up a new earth and a new city.

A World in Need of Healing

In many ways, the world we live in today is like the little girl in need of healing. We have real concerns about global warming and pollution. Wars continue to tear apart nations, cities, and families. In our world today, millions of people are suffering from natural disasters and drought. Many people find themselves without enough food, clean water, or decent shelter to keep them healthy. Many young children throughout the world are forced to work long hours to earn just a dollar or two a day. Political oppression is a reality for millions. At the root of so many ills in our world today is the failure of the human family to treat human life, especially that of the innocent and vulnerable, with the respect and dignity it deserves.

In our own country, and to some degree in your city or community, we have similar problems. Every community suffers from crime. Every city has citizens who don't have enough to eat and who sleep outside each night. In almost every community in America, human life is destroyed through the violence of abortion.

In such a world, what is Jesus sending us to do? Can we be healers and life givers, as he was?

How Do We Respond?

As Americans, we have the opportunity to respond to these and countless other concerns through our involvement in the political process. Jesus, who once gave hope to a family by raising a young girl from the dead, can give us hope today and help the human family experience new life. As followers of Jesus Christ, and as Catholics, we believe the Church has important things to say to us about how we can be a light for the people of our day and show them the way to new life.

In the following pages, you can explore a number of issues and how you, as a follower of Christ, can make your decision about which ballot issues and candidates you will support in the upcoming elections. No single person can solve the problems of the whole world alone, but how we vote and what we do in our own community, city, state, and nation does make a difference.

Chapter 1
The Church Community

"[Jesus] took the child's father and mother and those who were with him, and went in where the child was" (Mark 5:40). When Jesus healed a person, he did so with his disciples and others around him. One reason for this is that Jesus calls all of us to be part of a community. He speaks to each one of us in the depths of our heart and calls us to be his disciples and a people of God. This is the primary meaning of the word *Church*. The Church is a community of people first and a building second.

In the New Testament, the Book of Acts of the Apostles tells the story of how, after Christ ascended into heaven and sent the Holy Spirit to guide the Church, the followers of Christ grew in numbers. The disciples reached out to share the Good News of Jesus Christ with the larger community and contributed to the well-being of their fellow Christians. In all of this, it is clear that the Apostles, especially Saint Peter, guided the Church. We can confidently say that Saint Peter, with the guidance of the Holy Spirit and the help of his fellow Apostles, led the members of the early Church in living with the mind, heart, and hands of Christ.

The Pope and the other bishops of the world are the successors of Peter and the other Apostles, respectively. They continue to be the leaders of the Roman Catholic Church. Assisted by priests and deacons, they serve as a reminder of Christ's work of bringing healing and new life to our world, and they lead the people of God, just as Peter did, in living the mission of Christ. In this way, they guide the entire people, who constitute the Church, to do the same.

The Risen Christ has called you by name and chosen you through Baptism to do something great for God: to help bring about a new way of living. This is what Jesus means when he talks about God's Kingdom, or the Reign of God. Each of us is to demonstrate and invite others to live according to God's way, a way of life-giving presence or love. This is not something we do on our own. We do this through the gift of Christ's Spirit and as a member of the Church. We help bring about God's Reign when we act with love and treat others with dignity. We do this individually, but we also do it communally when we ensure that our local community promotes the dignity of all.

Church teaching provides a framework and method for helping us determine how to sort out the many issues we face today. This framework and method have their roots in the Scriptures and have been developed over the centuries. The Church's social teaching is passed on by the bishops, in union with the Pope. These leaders constitute the official teaching authority of the Church, also known as the *Magisterium*. In summary, the framework for the Church's social teaching rests on two pillars: (1) the dignity and respect for each human life, and (2) the common good of society.

Growth in Virtue as an Individual and as a Member of a Community

As Catholics, we are called to continually grow in virtue as individuals and as a community. Virtue can be described as moral excellence. In other words, we should continually strive to do and promote what is right and moral. Chapter 4 of this book offers a helpful process for making moral decisions.

To grow in virtue as Catholics, we must embrace two fundamental truths about all of us, as God's children. The first truth is that individually, each of us is one of God's beloved children. When we acknowledge that we are, as individuals, beloved by God, we are called to treat ourselves and others with dignity and respect from conception to natural death. This is not an area we can choose to support or not support. Church teaching is extremely clear in saying that all life is sacred and should be treated as such.

The second truth is that as a people, which includes each and every person in the world, we are God's holy people. This is not always easy to see, particularly when we encounter those with different beliefs or values than ours. The reality is that we are created to be a people of God and we have a responsibility to work for the betterment of all of God's children. For this reason, when we take action, we must look at not only the impact our decisions will have on our family, friends, and immediate community but also at the impact they will have on the state, national, and global community now and in the future.

Informing Your Conscience

Each of us has been blessed with a conscience. We often picture our conscience as a little voice in our heads that tells us what is right and wrong. Our conscience is, in fact, a gift from God that helps us make judgments based on practical reason. We have a responsibility to inform our conscience so we can make the best possible decisions. Being informed involves more than simply acting on the basis of our own opinions. First, we inform our conscience by recognizing the natural moral law within each of us—that is, our natural tendency, as humans, to desire what is right and good rather than what is evil. Second, we inform our conscience by embracing the Ten Commandments and the teachings of Jesus Christ. Third, we inform our conscience by embracing the truths offered through the teachings of the Catholic Church. When we use all these tools together to inform our conscience, we can be confident we will have a conscience that is in line with how God wants us to live our lives.

Violence and Peace

In our world, the majority of problems can be attributed to violence. Violence is the opposite of God's life-giving presence, God's love. Violence takes many forms. Gossiping about another person and teasing or bullying a person are forms of violence. Have you ever had something stolen from you? If so, you have been the victim of violence; you know what it feels like to be violated. A victim of date rape experiences great violence. A murder victim experiences great violence. The word *violence* can be substituted for the word *sin,* because violence separates us from the life God is calling us to lead.

The opposite of violence is peace. Peace is not simply the absence of conflict but is the result of right relationships that flow from love. When Jesus appeared to his disciples on Easter Sunday, his first word to them was "Peace." With that one word, he forgave them for denying and abandoning him. With that one word, he invited them to resume their relationship as loving friends. With that one word, he prepared them to go out to the ends of the earth and be witnesses to a new way of living by loving God and loving one's neighbor.

In our world today, the human family faces a stark choice: violence—whether it be domestic violence or the violence of terrorism—or peace. Christ has called you to speak "Peace" both in word and action. You do so first and foremost by the way you yourself speak and act. You can do this only by growing in virtue. Here's how Saint Paul put it:

> As God's chosen ones, holy and beloved, clothe yourselves with compassion, kindness, humility, meekness, and patience. Bear with one another and, if anyone has a complaint against another, forgive each other; just as the Lord has forgiven you, so you also must forgive. Above all, clothe yourselves with love, which binds everything together in perfect harmony. And let the peace of Christ rule in your hearts, to which indeed you were called in the one body. And be thankful. Let the word of Christ dwell in you richly; teach and admonish one another in all wisdom; and with gratitude in your heart sing psalms, hymns, and spiritual songs to God. And whatever you do, in word or deed, do everything in the name of the Lord Jesus, giving thanks to God the Father through him. (Colossians 3:12–17)

Promoting Peace Through Politics

You can promote peace by voting for candidates who are committed to making life better for others and for legislation that will enhance the greatest good for the greatest number of people. Sometimes because of the complexity of issues, or because a preferred candidate or piece of legislation seems to have little chance of winning, a person can feel like his or her vote won't count. The reality is that every vote counts. A few votes can make the difference between a candidate's winning or losing or legislation's passing or failing. Your vote can always be a way of sending the message that you want to promote peace and life-giving efforts.

Politics, in the best sense of the word, is the art of making real what will enhance the life of the greatest number of people in a diverse civil community. In a democratic society, every citizen of voting age has a responsibility to participate in the political process to help promote the well-being of society.

Chapter 2
You Are God's Beloved:
The Dignity of the Human Person

Guiding Vision

God wants all people to live in right relationships with one another and the world around them by truly loving one another and caring for creation. This is God's vision. Jesus called it God's Kingdom, God's Reign. Jesus embodied the Kingdom and spent his life making it a reality. That's why he raised up the little girl who died. That's why he forgave his disciples who, when everything seemed to fall apart at the time of his Crucifixion, ran away and denied him. Just as it took time for Jesus to teach his disciples how to heal and bring life, it takes time for us to learn what it means to be followers of Christ.

Part of being a follower of Christ is embracing Christ's teaching and the Church's teaching that each person, each life, has dignity and is sacred. Jesus taught this through his words and demonstrated it through his actions; the Church's teaching continues to proclaim this foundational principle. We each have been created by God as unique. We each have been blessed with a spirit that knows God. We each have been saved by the sacrifice of Jesus Christ. As you begin to look at the issues that will impact your votes, it is vital to recognize that all life has a dignity and is sacred from conception to natural death.

The Family

The family is the most basic unit of society and is the place where people first learn what it means to be part of a community and to respect the dignity of life. The role of the family is to nourish its individual members by helping them grow as healthy people, physically, mentally, emotionally, and in every other way. The family prepares its members to contribute to the well-being of the society they live in as well as the entire world. The family cannot do all this in and of itself. It is extended and supported by other institutions such as schools, businesses, local government, and the Church. Nothing, however, can take the place of a loving, healthy family nor provide certain things that only it can.

Today the family is facing a number of challenges. Parents may be stretched by the need for both of them to work outside the home, and many parents struggle to raise children alone. The frequency of domestic violence causes grave concern about the health of families. Perhaps the most fundamental challenge concerns the concept of marriage itself. Most Christian churches, and certainly the Catholic Church, understand that the ideal environment for children provides them with both a mother and a father, and that marriage is a union between a man and a woman.

The Church's understanding of marriage is rooted in the first story of Creation, where the author states:

> So God created humankind in his image,
> in the image of God he created them;
> male and female he created them.
> God blessed them, and God said to them, 'Be fruitful and multiply.'
> (Genesis 1:27–28)

The Gospel of Mark tells us that Jesus himself affirms this teaching when he says:

> "God made them male and female." "For this reason a man shall leave his father and mother and be joined to his wife, and the two shall become one flesh." So they are no longer two but one flesh. Therefore what God has joined together, let no one separate. (Mark 10:6–9)

The Catholic Church proclaims and supports this vision. God created humans male and female to compliment each other and to form a new whole: a family. Thus Church teaching opposes the promotion of same-sex unions as equivalent to the union of a man and woman in marriage. Church teaching clearly affirms the dignity and civil rights of people with a same-sex orientation but opposes making same-sex unions equal to marriage or even calling them marriages.

> When considering bills or positions of candidates, first determine what is being proposed. Ultimately the questions to ask are these: Will this bill or this candidate's position lead to the erosion of the ideal of marriage, which is a union between a man and a woman? Will it have a negative impact on family life? Catholic teaching tells us not to support candidates or legislation that promote same-sex unions as equal or equivalent to the marriage between a man and a woman.

Beginning of Life

The relationship between a man and a woman as husband and wife is unique and sacred. In the normal course of events, their love leads to the conception and birth of children. All creation is sacred to God. This is particularly true of human life. Baptism makes explicit what God says about every person: "You are my beloved daughter" or "You are my beloved son."

As one of God's beloved, each person has a dignity, preciousness, and sacredness that no one can take away. The dignity and sacredness of the human person as God's beloved are at the heart of the Church's teaching on human life. Today's disciples of Christ face many issues concerning the dignity of the individual and the sacredness of human life. Some of these, like abortion, are old. Some, like cloning and stem cell research, are new. Prior to voting, Catholics should learn all they can about ballot issues and candidates' positions on the issues.

Conception

In Matthew's Gospel, Jesus reminds his first listeners, and us as well, that from the very beginning, God created man and woman to be partners. Intercourse in marriage, between a man and a woman, is the normal way in which children are conceived and brought into this world (see Matthew 19:3–6).

Church teaching rejects all forms of artificial or assisted conception because they ultimately fail to promote the dignity of the parents and the child, especially because many embryos are destroyed or discarded in the process. From the first moment of conception, whether that takes place through normal intercourse or in a laboratory, the fertilized ovum is a human life with all the potential to become a person and is to be treated with care and dignity.

Cloning and Stem Cell Research

Some argue that life at its earliest stage should not be afforded the same degree of respect and protection as life at later stages. Some also argue that using embryonic stem cells to provide a cure for a disease—before individuality is present in that newly formed life—is morally acceptable. Church teaching emphasizes that *all* human life has dignity; destroying one life to cure disease in another does not promote dignity. Church teaching opposes any kind of embryonic stem cell research (manipulation of the fertilized ovum), including human cloning.

To treat human life as a commodity, as something to be manipulated, purchased, or destroyed—especially innocent human life—is morally wrong. It goes against who we are as God's beloved and as Christ's disciples. For this reason, the Catholic Church is clear in its teaching that embryonic stem cell research and human cloning are morally and seriously wrong.

> Issues that promote embryonic stem cell research or human cloning may be on a ballot in a given state. Carefully study these bills and the positions of candidates on these subjects. Because of the destruction of human life, Church teaching opposes embryonic stem cell research and human cloning.

Abortion

Abortion is the taking of human life while it is still in the mother's womb. In his encyclical letter *The Gospel of Life,* Pope John Paul II explains abortion this way: "Procured abortion is the deliberate and direct killing, by whatever means it is carried out, of a human being in the initial phase of his or her existence, extending from conception to birth" (no. 58).

From its earliest days, Church teaching has affirmed that procured abortion—abortion that is sought and obtained through direct or indirect means—is morally and seriously wrong (see *Catechism,* no. 2271). The letter of Barnabas says it plainly: "You shall not slay the child by procuring abortion; nor, again, shall you destroy it after it is born" *(Epistle of Barnabas).* This truth was reiterated by Pope John Paul II in his encyclical *The Gospel of Life:*

> The decision to have an abortion is often tragic and painful for the mother, insofar as the decision to rid herself of the fruit of conception is not made for purely selfish reasons or out of convenience, but out of a desire to protect certain important values such as her own health or a decent standard of living for the other members of the family. Sometimes it is feared that the child to be born would live in such conditions that it would be better if the birth did not take place. Nevertheless, these reasons and others like them, however serious and tragic, can never justify the deliberate killing of an innocent human being. (No. 58)

Catholic Church teaching on abortion is clear: It is morally and seriously wrong. Our goal must always be to eliminate abortions 100 percent. In our country today, and in our world, we can cooperate with others in reducing the number of abortions by providing pregnant women with more resources to assist them during pregnancy and in raising or letting others adopt their children. This can be done through political measures or through a variety of community efforts. Again it is important to look at ballot issues and candidates' positions.

It is important to also remember the need for reconciliation and compassion for those who have procured an abortion. In concluding his encyclical *The Gospel of Life,* Pope John Paul II spoke to women who have had abortions. This is what he said:

> I would like now to say a special word to women who have had an abortion. The Church is aware of the many factors which may have influenced your decision and she does not doubt that in many cases it was a painful and even shattering decision. The wound in your heart may not yet have healed. Certainly what happened was and remains terribly wrong. But do not give in to discouragement and do not lose hope. Try rather to understand what happened and face it honestly. If you have not already done so, give yourselves over with humility and trust to repentance. . . . With the friendly and expert help and advice from other people, and as a result of your own painful experience, you can be among the most eloquent defenders of

everyone's right to life. Through your commitment to life, whether by accepting the birth of other children or by welcoming and caring for those most in need of someone to be close to them, you will become promoters of a new way of looking at human life. (No. 99)

Pope John Paul II's words of compassion, forgiveness, and hope should guide us in our words and actions as we work to eliminate abortion in our land and promote the dignity of each human life, especially the lives of the unborn. When casting a vote for a candidate or a piece of legislation, make the protection of human life a priority. Take into consideration the issues that lead a person to seek an abortion and vote with those issues in mind as well.

End of Life

To be present at the birth of a child or the death of a loved one is to experience the mystery and gift of life in a most profound way. Perhaps you have heard this saying: "When a child is born, the child cries as it enters this world, but the child's parents and all present smile, laugh, and rejoice at the birth of a beautiful baby. When a person dies and is born into God's new world, everyone gathered around the deathbed cries, but he or she smiles, laughs, and rejoices at the sight of the Risen Christ and is fully embraced by the love of God."

As followers of Jesus Christ, we know death is not the end of life but a change in life. Our faith tells us that life, from a person's very first breath until his or her very last, is a gift. A person's life is complete when he or she makes a gift of his or her life back to God. In doing so, a healing of family and personal relationships that have been strained or broken often happens. Indeed death is, in reality, the beginning of new life.

Saint Ignatius described the gift of self well in one of his prayers:

> Take, O Lord, and receive my entire liberty,
> My memory, my understanding and my whole will.
> And all that I am and all that I possess You have given me:
> I surrender it all to you to be disposed of accordingly to Your will.
> Give me only Your love and Your grace;
> With these I will be rich enough,
> And will desire nothing more.
> Amen.

(Feast of All Saints Web site)

Euthanasia and Assisted Suicide

The Church teaches that euthanasia, "an act or omission which, of itself or by intention causes death, in order to eliminate suffering" is morally and seriously wrong (*Catechism*, no. 2277). The same can be said for assisted suicide, which provides a person, often one who has a terminal disease, with the means of ending her or his life. This too is seriously and morally wrong, for it is a failure to respect the gift of life given by God of which we are only stewards, not owners. Life is not ours to dispose of (see *Catechism*, no. 2280). Church teaching is consistent in its assertions that life is sacred from conception to natural death and should be treated as such. It is important to distinguish between euthansia and assisted sucide, which are direct actions or failures to act in order to cause a person to die, and withholding or withdrawing treatment in order to let death occur naturally.

> As Catholics, we are called to oppose the legalization of euthanasia and assisted suicide. At the same time, as followers of Jesus Christ, we need to support efforts to mitigate or even eliminate, with our loving presence and prayers, the physical pain and the psychological and spiritual sorrow of those who are dying.

Chapter 3
You Are God's Beloved People: The Common Good

Guiding Vision

We are individuals with a dignity, rights, and responsibilities that no one can take from us. At the same time, we are not isolated individuals. Each of us is a member of several communities. Each of us is a member of a family, a neighborhood, a parish, a town, a city, or a rural area. Each of us is a citizen of a state, the United States, and the world. Whatever the mixture of the various communities we belong to, the reality is that we benefit from and have a responsibility to enhance the common good of these communities. As stated earlier, it all begins in the home, where parents teach their growing children what it means to be a part of a community. When children grow up in a family with shared responsibilities, proper discipline, and structure, they learn what it means to be a part of a life-giving community and that they are expected to contribute to the common good.

The Common Good

The Church understands the common good to be "the sum total of social conditions which allow people, either as groups or as individuals, to reach their fulfillment more fully and more easily" (*Catechism*, no. 1906). The common good consists of three elements: (1) respect for the individual person, (2) the social well-being and development of the community itself, and (3) peace—the stability and security of a just order. The common good is always oriented toward the progress of persons. It is the role of the state to defend and promote the common good of civil society and its citizens. Today, because of the interdependence of people throughout the world, we can speak of a universal common good. (Adapted from *Catechism*, nos. 1907–1909)

Community Challenges

Every community, be it the family, the regional community, or the world, faces similar challenges. They occur on a different scale and with greater complexity on the world level than at the family level. The following chart illustrates and categorizes some of the major challenges communities face. Each category on the chart contains three issues meant to illustrate the challenges within the category. For example, one of the economic issues facing the world is global warming. The issues named on the chart are not the only issues affecting each community; instead, these are merely a sampling to help you begin looking at the challenges that impact all of God's children.

Perspective

The chart illustrates the connection among issues that affect the family, community, and world, although the relationship may not be direct. Not all issues are concerns with the same intensity, but they are all important, and we need to make an effort to determine the vision of those who are seeking elected office and the consequences of their stances on issues.

Church teaching supports the principle of subsidiarity. *Subsidiarity* means that what can be done at the local level should be done at that level. The expression "Think Globally, Act Locally" is an expression of this principle. Church teaching also makes it clear that the common good cannot be promoted unless, at the same time, the dignity of human life is protected and fostered.

In the following sections, we will look at specific topics under the categories of political issues, economic issues, and cultural issues. We will briefly examine the topics as they relate to families, regional communities, and the world. This will not be a complete examination of each topic but rather a sampling to help you learn to identify issues and the communities they impact.

	Family	Regional Community	World
Politically			
Conflict	domestic violence	crime	terrorism, war, and arms trade
Health Care	lack of clinics in urban or rural areas	lack of health insurance or retirement benefits	pandemics (AIDS, Avian Flu, etc.)
Human Rights	child neglect and abuse	discrimination and oppression	immigration and refugees
Economically			
Work	unemployment	denial of workers' right to organize	substandard working conditions
Poverty	homelessness	welfare reform	international debt
Ecology	widespread use of disposable products	toxic waste	global climate change
Culturally			
Education	lack of affordable child-care	unequal access to quality schools	denial of schooling for girls or for poor children
Media	children's exposure to violent or sexually charged content	pornography	loss of local culture
Religion	lack of freedom to worship	laws against public use of religious symbols	lack of religious tolerance

Political Issues

Conflict

Of all the issues communities face, conflict or violence is the most pervasive and destructive of the individual and the common good.

The Family

It all begins in the family. When a husband and wife love and respect each other, their children have the best opportunity of growing up with a healthy sense of identity, an appreciation of their gifts, and a willingness to make the world a better place. Too often, however, domestic violence between a husband and wife or between parents and their children or among children themselves afflicts families. Many times domestic abuse causes a cycle of abuse, where the abused later find themselves in other abusive relationships. Violence in the home can be exacerbated by the abuse of alcohol and drugs, which make it even harder for families to end the violence.

The Community

Like the family, the larger communities in which one lives provide opportunities for growth. One of the issues every community faces is what to do with those who commit crimes, especially serious crimes like murder. Ideally the treatment of criminals would provide for some measure of restitution and rehabilitation. For serious crimes, the community needs to decide whether capital punishment (putting the criminal to death) is the answer. In his encyclical *The Gospel of Life,* Pope John Paul II states:

> The nature and extent of the punishment must be carefully evaluated and decided upon, and ought not go to the extreme of executing the offender except in the case of absolute necessity. . . . Today, however, as a result of steady improvements in the organization of the penal system, such cases are very rare, if not practically non-existent. . . . If bloodless means are sufficient to defend human lives against an aggressor and to protect public order and the safety of persons, public authority must limit itself to such means, because they better

correspond to the concrete conditions of the common good and are more in conformity to the dignity of the human person. (No. 56)

In a consistent effort to promote the dignity of human life as well as the common good, Church teaching strongly recommends that capital punishment, especially in developed societies, be inflicted in only the rarest of situations. Additionally, we need to seek means to deal with crime and punishment that respect the dignity of both the victim and perpetrator.

The World

War is violence between nations. Though every effort is to be made to avoid war, every nation has a right to defend itself against an unjust aggressor. Church teaching acknowledges that there can be a "just war," but a number of conditions must be met (see *Catechism,* nos. 2307–2314). Pope John Paul II has stated "War is not always inevitable. It is always a defeat for humanity" ("Address of His Holiness Pope John Paul II to the Diplomatic Corps"). By that he meant war signifies the failure of nations to find alternative ways to resolve their differences.

Many related issues surround the issue of war: production and trade of weapons, nuclear war, preemptive war, terrorism, collateral damage, mines, unexploded cluster bombs, and so on. All of these eventually lead to destruction of property and the death of people.

> When voting, consider the candidates' positions on the prevention of domestic violence, crime, and capital punishment. We don't get a chance to vote on whether we as a nation should go to war, but our voice does make a difference to those who have the responsibility for doing so. We have the obligation to encourage leaders to exhaust every possible peaceful option to a conflict. There are serious moral concerns about preemptive or preventive use of force. It is vital to vote in a manner that promotes the well-being of the individual and the larger community.

Health Care

Adequate health care is an issue we, as a country, must address. Good health enables both individuals and communities to flourish. Health care is a fundamental human right. "We need to reform the nation's health care system, and this reform must be rooted in values that respect human dignity, protect human life, and meet the needs of the poor and uninsured" (United States Conference of Catholic Bishops [USCCB], *Faithful Citizenship*). Decent health care should be available to all, even those lacking health insurance or the financial means to pay for health care.

The quality of health care, the cost of prescription medication and medical services, and health insurance are complex issues. The questions of quality, coverage, and how much to spend for health care continue to be issues voters face in one way or another.

> When looking at the issue of health care, care of the aged, and insurance, we are called to first and foremost keep those in the direst situations in mind. How will legislation and political officials help those without the ability or resources to obtain adequate health care?

Human Rights

Unfortunately in our communities, country, and world, basic human rights are constantly infringed upon. Even though it violates our Christian values and is against the law, people in our country still suffer from racial discrimination. As individuals, as communities, and as a nation we, as Americans, should be leaders and set an example for others in the world in promoting respect and equal opportunities for all people, regardless of their race, creed, gender, sexual orientation, or nationality.

A significant human rights issue facing the nations of the world is immigration. Immigrants are those who move to a different country with the approval of that country. Immigrants often move to a new country seeking to improve their life. Undocumented immigrants are those who have moved to a different country without the required permission.

The Gospels compel us to "care for and stand with immigrants" (USCCB, *Faithful Citizenship*). Church teaching recognizes and affirms the right of a sovereign country to control its borders and regulate immigration. The United States bishops have stated that immigration laws need to be reviewed and, where appropriate, updated. With regard to the enforcement of immigration laws, the bishops have stated that efforts should be (1) *targeted* so that those who pose a risk to our country are intercepted, (2) *proportional* so that unnecessary penalties and force are avoided, and (3) *humane* so that a person's dignity and rights are preserved, families are not unduly separated, and a clear process for obtaining documentation in a reasonable amount of time is established. Additionally, we are called to look at the root causes of immigration and address, when possible, "the political, social and economic inequities that contribute" to immigration (USCCB, *Faithful Citizenship*).

> When looking at issues of human rights, keep the dignity of the human person first and foremost in your mind. Continued enforcement of laws against discrimination is a moral imperative. In relation to immigration, look for candidates who promote immigration laws that protect our country and the dignity and rights of immigrants.

Economic Issues

Work

It is true that work enables people to earn their living, but the goal of work should not be just earning money. It should be to enrich the life of the family and to enhance the life of the larger community by providing quality services and products.

Church teaching supports the right of every person to work and to know that he or she is making a contribution to the well-being of others. Every person has a right to a living wage, decent work conditions, and a workplace free of discrimination. Employees have a right to organize, if they choose, and bargain collectively for wages, benefits, and work conditions. Employers have a right to get an honest day's work from employees, have economic freedom, and operate in an open market.

As we increasingly become a more interconnected global community, we have the responsibility to expect fair treatment of workers around the world. When we support businesses that neglect the needs of their workers, we are giving approval to these kinds of immoral business practices. Standards and regulations for fair trade are in need of regular updates and enforcement. In addition, workers in other countries need to be fairly compensated for their work.

Chapter 3: You Are God's Beloved People: The Common Good

> When voting, keep in mind the rights of both the employees and the employers. Issues such as minimum wage increases, tax incentives for new businesses, and international trade policies need to be weighed in light of their benefit to the common good and their respect for the dignity of the person. Additionally, we as followers of Christ need to work for fair working conditions, fair wages, and fair trade policies in the global market place.

Poverty

For a wide variety of reasons, many individuals and families in America find themselves poor—so poor that they fall below the poverty line established by our own government. When people do not have decent housing or enough food or clothing, when they struggle to pay their utility bills or to buy needed medication, their well-being and the well-being of the larger community is in jeopardy. In our country, many charitable organizations make heroic efforts to provide food, clothing, and shelter for those who are in such need.

Every state and the federal government itself has developed programs to assist people who find themselves lacking the basic necessities of life. Any welfare reform should focus on reducing poverty and developing financial independence for the recipients of welfare. The focus should not be on cutting resources, programs, or funding. Welfare programs need to address the issues of work and career training, affordable and safe housing, child care, and health care.

Globally, poverty is at an appalling level. Many efforts are being made to assist people in obtaining the most basic necessities: clean drinking water, a consistent source of food, and decent housing. The poorest of the poor are those who are refugees, fleeing for their lives from oppression and war. We have a responsibility to work to improve the situations of those suffering from poverty around the world. We can do this by supporting candidates and legislation that will provide assistance to those in need around the world and by becoming personally involved in programs that assist those in need.

> We are called to vote for candidates and programs that will not only help meet the immediate needs of those suffering from poverty but that will also work to address the root causes of poverty, such as discrimination and lack of education.

Ecology

We know we need to live in harmony with our world. Pollution of the earth, the air, and the water is damaging the environment that we are commissioned by God to care for. The more we do to improve the condition of the environment, the better it will be for everyone today and for future generations.

Governments can set standards regarding emissions, be they from vehicles or from businesses. Known hazardous waste areas need to be cleaned up. Everyone can help make our environment clean, and local regulations can encourage them to do so. Everyone can become involved in recycling. Instead of using chemical-based fertilizers in their gardens and on their lawns, homeowners can use organic fertilizers. Farmers and ranchers can do likewise. These are just some steps that can be supported by local legislation. Both individual nations and the world community need to take action to provide for the continuing care of the environment, both locally and globally. These practical actions are real-life applications of Church teachings on the environment.

> Carefully examine the legislation and positions of candidates that relate to maintaining and developing a clean environment. As Catholics, we can support measures such as those that promote alternate, renewable, and clean-energy resources; those that address global climate change; and those that provide environmental assistance to poorer nations.

Cultural Issues

Education

The education of a child is a fundamental parental responsibility. The educational system exists to support the family and provide options for the education of a child. To this end, there should be educational options for children, including public, charter, and religious schools. The government should help provide resources for these schools, without discrimination, so parents can exercise their rights in selecting the best possible education for their children. Additionally, children should have schools where they feel safe to learn and are protected from violence.

> We are called to support parents' rights to choose the education best suited for their children and to ensure that resources are available for the quality education of all children. It is likely you will have the opportunity to vote for funding for school programs and school board elections. Examine the ballot issues and the positions of the candidates you are being asked to vote for in light of the necessity of a quality education for all children.

Communication

Cell phones, PDAs, and the Internet make it possible for a person to be in touch with what is happening throughout the world in just an instant. The rapid growth of technology is allowing us to be connected to one another and the world in ways unlike ever before. With this growth in technology, young people risk being exposed to material that is graphically inappropriate and harmful. Church teaching supports freedom of speech and the rights of parents and schools to protect children from inappropriate material.

Among the issues the larger community needs to address are the issues of violence and pornography. Depictions of violence and pornography promote the degradation of individuals and the quality of relationships among people. It is important to support the enforcement of existing obscenity and child pornography laws while supporting efforts to develop the technology for parents and schools to block unwanted material.

New technologies can expose children to other cultures, art, educational resources, and entertainment that can be of great benefit to their development. We must continue to support the development of technology and content that glorifies the dignity of the human person rather than degrades it.

> While supporting freedom of speech, we need to work to protect young people from violent and pornographic material that is more easily disseminated with the development of new technology. We need to support the development of technologies and laws that allow parents and schools to block and monitor children's use of technology. We must also support the enforcement of child pornography laws and other measures aimed at protecting young people.

Chapter 4
Making Decisions

Every four years since 1976, the United States Conference of Catholic Bishops has issued a statement on the responsibilities of Catholics to society. The 2004 edition of this statement, entitled *Faithful Citizenship,* summarizes, in a clear fashion, the consistent and challenging message found in Church teaching. The United States bishops remind all members of the Church of their responsibility to promote the dignity and sacredness of the human person and the common good. A new statement for the 2008 election is expected from the United States Conference of Catholic Bishops, so you should take the time to familiarize yourself with the new document when it is issued.

Social Teachings of the Catholic Church

The Church's social teachings arise out of the Scriptures and out of the Tradition of the Catholic Church. The vast, diverse, and daily lived experience of the Church helps focus and make concrete the social teachings of the Catholic faith. The major themes of the Church's social teaching can be summed up as follows:

- **Promoting the life and dignity of the human person.** "All human beings are sacred, from the time of conception until natural death, because they are created by God."
- **Supporting the common good at all levels: family, community, world.** "Human beings are social. They are called to live in community and to use their gifts for their own enrichment and for the common good."
- **Advocating for the rights and responsibilities of people.** "Human beings have rights in accordance with their dignity as children of God. Each right carries a corresponding responsibility."

- **Promoting the dignity of work and the rights of workers.** "Work is not simply a commodity to be exchanged for a wage. Workers share in God's creative action and have a right to a living wage."
- **Choosing to provide for the poor and vulnerable.** "As long as serious inequalities exist in allocation of power and resources, Christians are called to give particular care to those who have less."
- **Developing solidarity with people throughout the world.** "God's love is not limited by barriers of race, nation, or geographical distance. People are all responsible for one another."
- **Caring for God's creation.** "The universe is created by God and loaned to people for their prudent use. They are to be good stewards of creation, mindful of generations to follow."

(Constance Fourré, *Journey to Justice,* pp. 6–7)

In a clear, consistent, and challenging manner, the teaching authority of the Church presents the message to its people and politicians that we are to work to protect the dignity of life, to promote peace in the world, and to be advocates for justice in all that we do. As Catholics, we have a responsibility to work to address all these social justice themes in how we live our lives, how we interact with others, and how we express ourselves in the political process. Among these issues though, the right to life is preeminent because without life there can be no human development.

Whom to Vote For? What Ballot Issues to Vote For?

Guided by the teachings of the Church and our conscience, we are presented with these questions: Whom do I vote for, and what ballot issues do I choose to support or oppose? Because it is rare to find a candidate whose positions are 100 percent in agreement with the Church's moral vision, or ballot issues that adequately cover a particular Church teaching, voting becomes complex. Some issues are easier to discern, like voting to repair roads or to fund schools. Other issues involve more serious moral matters, such as whether to approve assisted suicide.

Making Moral Decisions

The process of making a moral decision begins with an understanding of who we are and what we are called to do. We are each one of God's beloved daughters or sons. We are disciples of the Risen Christ. As such, we have been commissioned to carry on the work of Christ today. Just as Christ brought life to the little girl and the people of his day, so we are to bring life to the people and communities of our day. Knowing who we are and that we are called to share in Christ's own mission, we can make decisions about how we should act. Our decisions and actions are either moral or immoral.

The word *morality* comes from the Latin word *moralis* meaning custom. Morality has to do, then, with the way one customarily acts. How should a Christian act? One who follows Christ should act as Christ acted. How did Christ act? Christ acted as God the Father acts: bringing about goodness, order, and life.

Jesus Christ has not left us orphans but has given us his Spirit and the Christian community (the Church) to guide us in our actions; we are not called to act alone but in union with Christ and our fellow disciples. Thus we must act with an informed conscience. The word *conscience* refers to the ability to make a judgment that something is or is not in keeping with who we are and our mission as Christ's disciples. To be informed is not to act simply on the basis of our own opinions; rather, we are informed by our relationship with Christ and his disciples, the Church. To act with an informed conscience is a shorthand way of saying to act in union with Christ through prayer and the presence of the Spirit. We need to be in union with the Church by knowing that Church teaching promotes certain values and principles and why it promotes them.

A Basic Approach

Christians often find themselves facing a situation in which there is a conflict of values, most often a choice between one set of goods and another set of goods. How is one to make a decision when faced with such a conflict? It is helpful to first identify a basic approach and then the issue of the upcoming elections:

- Know who you are and that you have a mission.
- Hold clearly in your mind and heart the ideal that Christ and the Church are calling us to bring life to people and communities by promoting the dignity of each person's life and the common good of each community.
- Know the principles and values applicable to the current situation. These come from the Bible and the experience of the Christian community. In the early Church, the Apostles officially articulated these. Today the successors to the Apostles, the bishops, articulate them.
- Consult with experts to clearly understand the situation and the probable consequences of a specific course of action.
- Pray for guidance from the Lord and the Spirit.
- Given all the circumstances, make the best decision possible so that as many values as possible might be achieved.
- Participate in the political process so that future progress might be made.
- Vote responsibly. At appropriate times, sending letters, e-mails, or faxes to elected officials or candidates can be effective. You might decide to become involved with a particular party or candidate in preparation for future elections.

Questions and Answers

Why in the presidential election of 2004 did some bishops say that certain Catholic candidates could not receive Communion?

In the presidential election of 2004, several bishops stated that Catholic politicians who were pro-choice or who advocated embryonic stem cell research, euthanasia, or same-sex marriages had placed themselves outside of the Church and therefore should not receive Communion until they were reconciled with the Church. In addition, some said that Catholics who voted for such politicians were similarly outside the Church. In the fall of 2006, the United States bishops, as a body, wrote a pastoral letter entitled "Happy Are Those Who Are Called to His Supper," in which they discuss the importance of receiving Communion worthily.

How might one summarize the teachings in "Happy Are Those Who Are Called to His Supper"?

In their teaching role, bishops sometimes act in the tradition of the prophets, who stated, "THUS SAYS THE LORD!" Such statements are clear and unambiguous. The bishops who spoke out in 2004 caused both candidates and voters to take a serious look at their responsibilities as Catholics and citizens.

The bishops make every effort to present in a clear, consistent, and challenging way the message of the Gospel and the Church. This is the approach they took in their 2006 letter "Happy Are Those Who Are Called to His Supper." This approach encourages dialogue with those in public office and with the community itself.

This approach also recognizes that there are a variety of legitimate judicial, legislative, and cultural strategies for promoting the sacredness of human life (limiting the tragedy of abortion, euthanasia, and so on) and the common good. It places the burden for making the decision to receive or not to receive Communion on those involved. As Saint Paul said, "Whoever, therefore, eats the bread or drinks the cup of the Lord in an unworthy manner will be answerable for the body and blood of the Lord. Examine yourselves, and only then eat of the bread and drink of the cup" (1 Corinthians 11:27–28).

What are we to make of Catholic politicians who say they are personally against abortion but support pro-choice legislation?

Catholic politicians and voters are called to be supportive of the "seamless garment of life." This includes support for all the pro-life issues and the promotion of the common good. Catholic politicians have an obligation to be clear that they are pro-life and that they are not just using those words to get votes. Voters need to understand that, depending on the office, there are limits to what elected officials can do, and there are different strategies for promoting the sacredness and dignity of human life.

As a Catholic voter, am I out of communion with the Church if I vote for a candidate who is pro-choice?

If a voter were to vote for a candidate primarily because she or he were pro-choice, then the answer would be yes. If a voter were to determine that such a candidate would be effective in promoting the sacredness of life and the overall well-being of those she or he would serve, the answer would be no. Should this be the case, the voter should communicate with the candidate and explain why she or he voted for this candidate but also explain her or his conviction of the importance of promoting the dignity of each person's life and the common good.

What if I don't want to vote for any of the candidates for a given position? Is it wrong not to vote?

Voting is a serious obligation. Should you choose not to vote, you still have a responsibility to work for the common good. For example, you could write to each candidate explaining your decision to not vote and encouraging the candidates to modify their positions.

Why does the Church get involved in politics?

As followers of Jesus Christ, we are called to proclaim in word and action the Good News of God's Reign. We can sum it up by saying we are to promote goodness, order, and life for all people. We are to do this everyday, everywhere, and at every time. The Church proclaims an ultimate vision and encourages all to help in making that vision a reality. The Church would fail in its mission if it did not speak to the community at the times the community is making important decisions about how to live together.

Is the Catholic Church telling me how to vote?

The Catholic Church does not tell its members how to vote. The Church reminds all Catholics that the promotion of human life and the common good of all people are foundational to the long-term well-being of society. Politicians and voters alike have a moral responsibility to promote these values.

Is there a single issue where a candidate's position would prevent a Catholic from voting for that person (such as a pro-choice stance)?

Even though some bishops and some individuals in the Church would answer that question yes, the bishops, as a body, do not support the idea of a single issue litmus test. Church teaching, through Pope John Paul II's encyclical on human life, titled "Evangelium Vitae," and through the United States Conference of Catholic Bishops' *Faithful Citizenship*, makes it clear that voters have a serious moral responsibility to study all the issues and candidates and then vote for the candidate they think would best advance the dignity of human life and the common good.

The Long Haul

"Little girl, get up!" When Jesus raised the little girl back to life, he showed that he was the fulfillment of God's Promise. That Promise is the promise of life. God wants each person and each community to experience life now. We will not experience the fullness of life until the time of God's new world, but, to the extent that we love one another as Jesus taught us, we can experience that life now.

Faithful Citizen, Faithful Catholic is just the beginning of your process of informing your conscience and your vote. You must now take the next steps. These include informing yourself about the politicians and legislation you will have the opportunity to vote on, spending time reading and discussing the teachings of the Catholic Church, and praying for guidance to cast votes that protect the dignity of human life and promote the common good.

Sometimes it seems as if life will not triumph, but God has promised otherwise. We must keep this vision in our hearts and act with integrity and dignity in our daily lives. If we are faithful to being life givers to our neighbors and to our communities today, the Spirit of God will ensure that God's life will triumph.

Acknowledgments

The scriptural quotations contained herein are from the New Revised Standard Version of the Bible, Catholic Edition. Copyright © 1993 and 1989 by the Division of Christian Education of the National Council of the Churches of Christ in the United States of America. All rights reserved.

The quotations on pages 16, 17, 17–18, and 23–24 are from *The Gospel of Life (Evangelium vitae)*, numbers 58, 58, 99, and 56, respectively, at *www.vatican.va/holy_father/john_paul_ii/encyclicals/documents/hf_jp-ii_enc_25031995_evangelium-vitae_en.html*, accessed March 20, 2007.

The quotation on page 16 is from *Epistle of Barnabas*, at *www.newadvent.org/fathers/0124.htm*, accessed March 20, 2007.

The Saint Ignatius prayer on page 18 is from the Feast of All Saints Web site, at *www.feastofsaints.com/threeofignatius.htm*, accessed March 22, 2007.

The excerpts on pages 19 and 20 are from the English translation of the *Catechism of the Catholic Church* for use in the United States of America, numbers 2277 and 1906. Copyright © 1994 by the United States Catholic Conference, Inc.—Libreria Editrice Vaticana. Used with permission.

The quotation on page 24 is from "Address of His Holiness Pope John Paul II to the Diplomatic Corps," at *www.vatican.va/holy_father/john_paul_ii/speeches/2003/january/documents/hf_jp-ii_spe_20030113_diplomatic-corps_en.html*, accessed March 20, 2007.

The excerpts on pages 24–25, 25, and 26 are from *Faithful Citizenship: A Catholic Call to Political Responsibility*, by the United States Conference of Catholic Bishops, at *www.usccb.org/faithfulcitizenship/bishopStatement.html*, accessed March 20, 2007.

The principles listed on pages 31–32 are from *Journey to Justice: Transforming Hearts and Schools with Catholic Social Teaching*, by Constance Fourré (Washington, DC: National Catholic Educational Association [NCEA], 2003), pages 6–7. Copyright © 2003 by NCEA. Used with permission.

To view copyright terms and conditions for Internet materials cited here, log on to the home pages for the referenced Web sites.

During this book's preparation, all citations, facts, figures, names, addresses, telephone numbers, Internet URLs, and other pieces of information cited within were verified for accuracy. The authors and Saint Mary's Press staff have made every attempt to reference current and valid sources, but we cannot guarantee the content of any source, and we are not responsible for any changes that may have occurred since our verification. If you find an error in, or have a question or concern about, any of the information or sources listed within, please contact Saint Mary's Press.